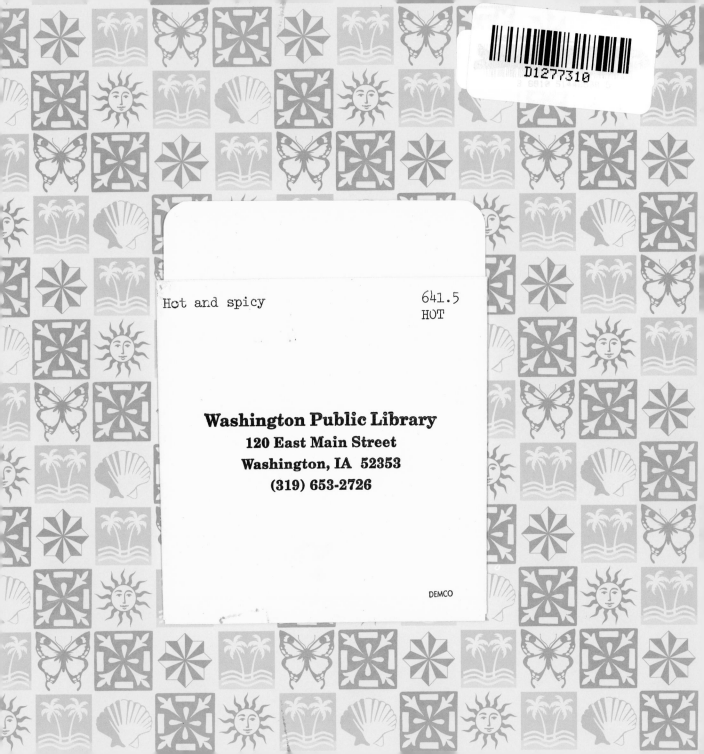

HOT AND SPICY

★ ★ FIERY FAVORITES FROM AMERICA'S HOT SPOTS ★ ★

HOT AND SPICY

✯ ✯ FIERY FAVORITES FROM AMERICA'S HOT SPOTS ✯ ✯

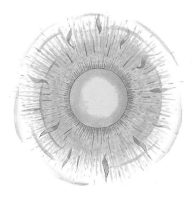

CONSULTANT EDITOR: LINDLEY BOEGEHOLD

SMITHMARK

This edition published in 1995 by
SMITHMARK Publishers Inc.
16 East 32nd Street
New York, NY 10016

SMITHMARK books are available for bulk purchase for sales promotion and for premium use.
For details write or call the Manager of Special Sales, SMITHMARK Publishers Inc., 16 East 32nd Street,
New York, NY, 10016; (212) 532-6600.

ISBN 0 8317 7455 X

Publisher: Joanna Lorenz
Editorial Manager: Helen Sudell
Designer: Nigel Partridge
Photographer: Amanda Haywood and P. R. Dunn, Picture Perfect, USA (pp 6/7)
Recipes by: Carla Capalbo and Laura Washburn
Illustrations by: Estelle Corke

Printed and bound in Singapore

Contents

" A CHILI WREATH HANGING ON THE WALL
GIVES HEAT AND HEART TO ONE AND ALL

A CHILI PEPPER IN THE POT
SPICES, ENTICES AND MAKES THE STEW HOT."
ANON

"I NEVER MET A CHILI PEPPER I DIDN'T LIKE."
ANCHO CHILI BILL

TORTILLA SOUP

—

CRUNCHY TORTILLAS, SMOOTH AVOCADO AND FRESH HERBS GIVE THIS ZESTY SOUP AN EXCITING
TEXTURE. MOM'S CHICKEN SOUP NEVER TASTED SO GOOD.

8

SERVES 4-6

1 tablespoon vegetable oil

1 onion, minced

1 large garlic clove, minced

2 medium tomatoes, peeled, seeded, and chopped

½ teaspoon salt

2 quarts chicken stock

1 carrot, diced

1 small zucchini, diced

1 skinless boneless chicken breast half, cooked and
    shredded

¼ cup canned green chilies, chopped

FOR GARNISHING

4 corn tortillas

oil for frying

1 small ripe avocado

2 scallions, chopped

chopped fresh cilantro

shredded Monterey Jack cheese (optional)

Heat the oil in a saucepan. Add the onion and garlic and cook over medium heat until just softened, 5-8 minutes. Add the tomatoes and salt and cook 5 minutes more.

Stir in the stock. Bring to a boil, then lower the heat and simmer, covered, about 15 minutes.

Meanwhile, for the garnish, trim the tortillas into squares, then cut them into strips.

Put a ½ inch layer of oil in a skillet and heat until hot but not smoking. Add the tortilla strips, in batches, and fry until just beginning to brown, turning occasionally. Remove with a slotted spoon and drain on paper towels.

Add the carrot to the soup. Cook, covered, 10 minutes. Add the zucchini, chicken, and chilies and continue cooking, uncovered, until the vegetables are just tender, about 5 minutes more.

Meanwhile, peel and pit the avocado. Chop into a fine dice.

Divide the tortilla strips among 4 soup bowls. Sprinkle with the chopped avocado. Ladle in the soup, then scatter scallions and cilantro on top. Serve immediately, adding the shredded Monterey Jack cheese if desired.

COOK'S TIP

PACKAGED TORTILLAS ARE READILY AVAILABLE FROM
LARGER SUPERMARKETS.

SPICY BEAN SOUP

—

THIS HEARTY SOUP HAS BEEN LIBERALLY SPICED AND DRESSED UP WITH CILANTRO AND SOUR CREAM. IF YOU ARE PRESSED FOR TIME CANNED BEANS MAY BE USED INSTEAD.

10

SERVES 6-8

1 cup dried black beans, soaked overnight and
*   drained*
1 cup dried kidney beans, soaked overnight and
*   drained*
2 bay leaves
3 tablespoons coarse salt
2 tablespoons olive or vegetable oil
3 carrots, chopped
1 onion, chopped
1 celery stalk, chopped
1 garlic clove, minced
1 teaspoon ground cumin
¼-½ teaspoon cayenne
½ teaspoon dried oregano
salt and pepper
⅓ cup red wine
1 quart beef stock
1 cup water

FOR GARNISHING
sour cream
chopped fresh
*   cilantro*

Put the black beans and kidney beans in two separate pots. Add a bay leaf to each and cover with cold water. Bring to a boil, then cover, and simmer 30 minutes.

Add 3 tablespoons coarse salt to each pot and continue simmering until the beans are tender, about 30 minutes. Drain and let cool slightly. Discard bay leaves.

Heat the oil in a large flameproof casserole. Add the carrots, onion, celery, and garlic and cook over low heat, stirring, until softened, 8-10 minutes. Stir in the cumin, cayenne, oregano, and salt to taste.

Add the wine, stock, and water and stir to mix. Add the beans. Bring to a boil, reduce the heat, then cover and simmer about 20 minutes, stirring occasionally.

Transfer half of the soup (including most of the solids) to a food processor or blender. Process until smooth. Return to the pan and stir to combine well.

Reheat the soup if necessary and taste for seasoning. Serve hot, garnished with sour cream and chopped fresh cilantro.

ARIZONA JALAPEÑO-ONION QUICHE

—

HOT PEPPERS GIVE BITE TO THIS SOUTHWESTERN TWIST ON A FRENCH
CLASSIC. SERVE IT WITH FRESH TORTILLAS AND A GREEN SALAD FOR A DESERT
BISTRO LUNCH.

12

SERVES 6

1 tablespoon butter

2 onions, sliced

4 scallions, cut in ½ inch pieces

½ teaspoon ground cumin

1-2 tablespoons chopped canned jalapeños

4 eggs

1¼ cups milk

½ teaspoon salt

⅔ cup shredded Monterey Jack or cheddar cheese

FOR THE CRUST

1½ cups flour

¼ teaspoon salt

¼ teaspoon cayenne

6 tablespoons cold butter

6 tablespoons cold margarine

2-4 tablespoons ice water

For the crust, sift the flour, salt, and cayenne into a bowl. Cut in the butter and margarine until the mixture resembles coarse meal. Sprinkle with 2 tablespoons ice water and mix until the dough holds together. If the dough is too crumbly, add a little more water, 1 tablespoon at a time. Gather the dough and flatten into a disk. Wrap the dough in wax paper and refrigerate at least 30 minutes.

Preheat the oven to 375°F.

Roll out the dough to a thickness of about ⅛ inch. Use to line a 9-inch fluted tart pan that has a removable base. Prick the bottom of the quiche shell all over with a fork. Line the shell with wax paper and fill with dried beans.

Bake until the pastry has just set, 12-15 minutes. Remove from the oven and carefully lift out the paper and beans. Prick the bottom of the pastry shell all over. Return to the oven and bake until golden, 5-8 minutes more. Leave the oven on.

Melt the butter in a nonstick skillet. Add the onions and cook over medium heat until softened, about 5 minutes. Add the scallions and cook 1 minute more. Stir in the cumin and jalapeños and set aside.

In a mixing bowl, combine the eggs, milk, and salt and whisk until thoroughly blended.

Spoon the onion mixture into the pastry shell. Sprinkle with cheese, then pour in the egg mixture.

Bake until the filling is golden and set, 30-40 minutes. Serve hot or at room temperature.

SAN ANTONIO TORTILLA

—

THINK OF THIS AS A TEXAS PIZZA. ITS BIG BOLD FLAVOR WORKS EQUALLY WELL AT BRUNCH, LUNCH OR DINNER. JUST VARY THE ACCOMPANIMENTS.

14

SERVES 4

1 tablespoon vegetable oil

½ onion, sliced

1 small green bell pepper, seeded and sliced

1 garlic clove, minced

1 tomato, chopped

6 black olives, chopped

3 small potatoes (about 10 ounces total), cooked and sliced

2 ounces sliced chorizo, cut in strips

1 tablespoon chopped canned jalapeños, or to taste

½ cup shredded cheddar cheese

6 extra large eggs

3 tablespoons milk

½ - ¾ teaspoon salt

¼ teaspoon ground cumin

¼ teaspoon dried oregano

¼ teaspoon paprika

black pepper

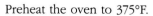

Preheat the oven to 375°F.

Heat the oil in a nonstick skillet. Add the onion, bell pepper, and garlic and cook over medium heat until softened, 5-8 minutes.

Transfer the vegetables to a 9-inch round non-stick cake pan. Add the tomato, olives, potatoes, chorizo, and jalapeños. Sprinkle with the cheese.

In a bowl, combine the eggs and milk and whisk until frothy. Add the salt, cumin, oregano, paprika, and pepper to taste. Whisk to blend.

Pour the egg mixture into the vegetable mixture, tilting the pan to spread it evenly (see above).

Bake until set and lightly golden, about 30 minutes. Serve immediately.

COOK'S TIP

THIS DISH ALSO TASTES GOOD COLD, SO IS PERFECT FOR TAKING ON PICNICS.

CHILES RELLENOS

POBLANO PEPPERS USED HERE ARE A RELATIVELY MILD CHILI, BUT HAVE A BIT MORE BITE THAN BELL PEPPERS. IF USING BELL PEPPERS INSTEAD OF POBLANOS, ADD SOME ZIP WITH ½ TO 1 TEASPOON OF HOT CHILI POWDER.

16

SERVES 4

*8 large green bell peppers or fresh green chilies
    such as poblano*
1-2 tablespoons vegetable oil, plus more for frying
4 cups shredded Monterey Jack cheese
4 eggs, separated
⅔ cup flour

FOR THE SAUCE

1 tablespoon vegetable oil
1 small onion, minced
¼ teaspoon salt
1-2 teaspoons red pepper flakes
½ teaspoon ground cumin
1 cup beef or chicken stock
3 cups canned peeled tomatoes

For the sauce, heat the oil in a skillet. Add the onion and cook over low heat until just soft, about 8 minutes. Stir in the salt, pepper flakes, cumin, stock, and tomatoes. Cover and simmer gently 5 minutes, stirring occasionally.

Transfer to a food processor or blender and process until smooth. Strain into a clean pan. Taste for seasoning, and set aside.

Preheat the broiler.

Brush the bell peppers or chilies lightly with oil. Lay them on a baking sheet. Broil as close to the heat as possible until blackened all over, 5-8 minutes. Cover with a clean dishtowel and set aside.

When cool enough to handle, remove the charred skin. Carefully slit the peppers or chilies and scoop out the seeds (and white veins for less chili heat). If using chilies, wear rubber gloves.

With your hands, form the cheese into 8 cylinders that are slightly shorter than the peppers. Place the cheese cylinders inside the peppers. Secure the slits with wooden toothpicks. Set aside.

Beat the egg whites until just stiff. Add the egg yolks, one at a time, beating on low speed just to incorporate them. Beat in 1 tablespoon of the flour.

Put a 1-inch layer of oil in a skillet or frying pan. Heat until hot but not smoking (drop a scrap of batter in the oil: if the oil sizzles, it is ready for frying).

Coat the peppers lightly in flour all over; shake off any excess. Dip into the egg batter, then place in the hot oil. Fry until brown on one side, about 2 minutes. Turn carefully and brown the other side.

Reheat the sauce and serve immediately with the chiles rellenos.

CAJUN BLACKENED SWORDFISH

—

PAUL PRUD'HOMME INVENTED THIS DRAMATIC, ALMOST INSTANTANEOUS METHOD OF PREPARING
FISH FILLETS. MAKE SURE YOU HAVE THE WINDOWS OPEN WHEN YOU PREPARE THIS NEW CAJUN
CLASSIC — THE SEARING OF THE FISH GENERATES CLOUDS OF SMOKE.

SERVES 4

1 teaspoon onion powder

1 teaspoon garlic salt

2 teaspoons paprika

1 teaspoon ground cumin

1 teaspoon mustard powder

1 teaspoon cayenne

2 teaspoons dried thyme

2 teaspoons dried oregano

½ teaspoon salt

1 teaspoon pepper

4 swordfish steaks (about 1½ pounds)

4 tablespoons butter or margarine, melted

dill sprigs, for garnishing

In a small bowl, combine all the spices, herbs, and seasonings.

Brush both sides of the fish steaks with a little butter or margarine.

Coat both sides of the fish steaks with the seasoning mixture, rubbing it in well.

Heat a large heavy skillet until a drop of water sprinkled on the surface sizzles, about 5 minutes.

Drizzle 2 teaspoons of the remaining butter or margarine over the fish steaks. Add the steaks to the skillet, butter-side down, and cook until the underside is blackened, 2-3 minutes.

Drizzle another 2 teaspoons melted butter or margarine over the fish (see above), then turn the steaks over.

Continue cooking until the second side is blackened and the fish flakes easily when tested with a fork, about 2-3 minutes more.

Transfer the fish to warmed plates, garnish with dill, and drizzle with the remaining butter or margarine.

RED SNAPPER WITH CILANTRO SALSA

—

OUR DESIRE TO CUT DOWN ON FATS HAS CAUSED FISH CONSUMPTION TO RISE. THIS DELECTABLE
SAUCE PROVES THAT FISH DOESN'T HAVE TO BE SERVED PLAIN TO BE HEALTHY.

SERVES 4

4 red snapper fillets (about 6 ounces)
salt and pepper
1½ tablespoons vegetable oil
1 tablespoon butter

FOR THE SALSA

2 cups fresh cilantro leaves
1 cup olive oil
2 garlic cloves, chopped
2 tomatoes, cored and chopped
2 tablespoons fresh orange juice
1 tablespoon sherry vinegar
1 teaspoon salt

 For the salsa, place the cilantro, oil, and garlic in a food processor or blender. Process until almost smooth. Add the tomatoes and pulse on and off several times; the mixture should remain slightly chunky and not too smooth.

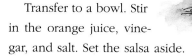

Transfer to a bowl. Stir in the orange juice, vinegar, and salt. Set the salsa aside.

Rinse the fish fillets and pat dry. Sprinkle on both sides with salt and pepper. Heat the oil and butter in a large nonstick skillet. When hot, add the fish and cook until opaque throughout, 2-3 minutes on each side (see left). Work in batches, if necessary.

Carefully transfer the fillets to warmed dinner plates. Top each with a spoonful of salsa. Serve additional salsa on the side.

COOK'S TIP

IF YOU CAN'T BUY RED SNAPPER, ANY FIRM WHITE FISH FILLETS, SUCH AS GROUPER, ORANGE ROUGHY OR MAHI MAHI WILL DO JUST AS WELL.

CORNMEAL-COATED GULF SHRIMP

—

MAKE TWICE AS MANY OF THESE SHRIMP AS YOU THINK YOU'LL NEED; THEY ARE ADDICTIVE.

SERVES 4

¾ cup cornmeal

1-2 teaspoons cayenne

½ teaspoon ground cumin

1 teaspoon salt

2 tablespoons chopped fresh cilantro or parsley

2 pounds large raw Gulf shrimp, peeled and
  deveined

flour, for dredging

¼ cup vegetable oil

1 cup shredded Monterey Jack or cheddar cheese

FOR SERVING

lime wedges

tomato salsa

Preheat the broiler.

In a bowl, combine the cornmeal, cayenne, cumin, salt, and cilantro or parsley.

Coat the shrimp lightly in flour, then dip in water and roll in the cornmeal mixture to coat.

Heat the oil in a nonstick skillet. When hot, add the

shrimp, in batches if necessary. Cook until they are opaque throughout, 2-3 minutes on each side (see above). Drain on paper towels.

Place the shrimp in a large baking dish, or individual dishes. Sprinkle the cheese evenly over the top. Broil about 3 inches from the heat until the cheese melts, 2-3 minutes. Serve immediately, with lime wedges and salsa.

> **COOK'S TIP**
>
> USE ONLY THE FRESHEST SHRIMPS IN YOUR COOKING.
> SHRIMPS DETERIORATE BADLY AFTER POOR HANDLING
> OR LONG STORAGE.

JAMBALAYA

—

THIS CLASSIC CAJUN DISH IS FANTASTIC FOR BIG PARTIES: SERVE IT IN BOWLS WITH LOTS OF
CRUSTY BREAD ON THE SIDE.

SERVES 6

2 tablespoons corn oil

*4 skinless boneless chicken breast halves, cut into
    chunks*

1 pound spicy cooked sausage, sliced

6 ounces smoked ham, cubed

1 large onion, chopped

2 celery stalks, chopped

2 green bell peppers, seeded and chopped

3 garlic cloves, minced

2 cups chicken stock

1 cup canned crushed tomatoes

1 teaspoon cayenne

1 sprig of fresh thyme or ¼ teaspoon dried thyme

2 sprigs of Italian parsley

1 bay leaf

1½ cups rice

salt and pepper

4 scallions, finely chopped

Heat the oil in a large frying pan. Add the chicken chunks and sausage slices and cook until well browned, about 5 minutes. Stir in the ham cubes and cook 5 minutes longer.

Add the onion, celery, bell peppers, garlic, stock, tomatoes, cayenne, thyme, parsley, and bay leaf to the frying pan. Bring to a boil, stirring well.

Stir in the rice, and season to taste (see above). When the liquid returns to a boil, reduce the heat and cover the pan tightly. Simmer 10 minutes.

Remove the pan from the heat and, without removing the lid, set aside for 20 minutes, to let the rice finish cooking.

Discard the bay leaf. Garnish the jambalaya by scattering the chopped scallions on top just before serving.

BLACK BEAN BURRITOS

—

BURRITOS ARE A WONDERFUL VEHICLE FOR ALL SORTS OF FILLINGS. YOU CAN SUBSTITUTE
SHREDDED CHICKEN, PORK OR SEAFOOD — THEY WILL ALL BE DELICIOUS.

26

SERVES 4

1 cup dried black beans, soaked overnight and
   drained
1 bay leaf
3 tablespoons coarse salt
1 small red onion, minced
2 cups shredded Monterey Jack cheese
1-3 tablespoons chopped pickled jalapeños
1 tablespoon chopped fresh cilantro
3½ cups tomato salsa
8 flour tortillas
diced avocado, for serving

Place the beans in a large pot. Add the bay
leaf and fresh cold water to cover. Bring to
a boil, then cover, and simmer 30 minutes. Add the
salt and continue simmering until tender, about 30
minutes more. Drain and let cool slightly.
Discard the bay leaf.
Preheat the oven to 350°F.
Grease a rectangular
baking dish.
In a bowl, combine
the beans, onion,
half the cheese, the
jalapeños, cilantro, and 1 cup of
the salsa. Stir to blend and taste
for seasoning.

Place 1 tortilla on a work surface. Spread a large
spoonful of the filling down the middle, then roll up
to enclose the filling (see below). Place the burrito
in the prepared dish, seam side down. Repeat with
the remaining tortillas.

Sprinkle the remaining cheese over the burritos,
in a line down the middle. Bake until the cheese
melts, about 15 minutes.

Arrange the diced avocado and the remaining
salsa mixture on warmed plates. Add the burritos
and serve immediately.

GALVESTON CHICKEN

—

28

SERVES 4

3½ pound chicken

juice of 1 lemon

4 garlic cloves, minced

1 tablespoon cayenne

1 tablespoon paprika

1 tablespoon dried oregano

½ teaspoon coarse black pepper

2 teaspoons olive oil

1 teaspoon salt

With a sharp knife or poultry shears, remove the backbone from the chicken. Turn it breast side up. With the heel of your hand, press down to break the breastbone, and open the chicken flat like a book. Insert a skewer through the chicken, at the thighs, to keep it flat during cooking.

Place the chicken in a shallow dish and pour over the lemon juice.

In a small bowl, combine the garlic, cayenne, paprika, oregano, pepper, and oil. Mix well. Rub evenly over the chicken (see below left).

Cover and let marinate 2-3 hours at room temperature, or refrigerate overnight (return to room temperature before roasting).

Season the chicken with salt on both sides. Transfer it to a shallow roasting pan.

Put the pan in a cold oven and set the temperature to 400°F. Roast until the chicken is done, about 1 hour, turning occasionally and basting with the pan juices. To test for doneness, prick with a skewer: the juices that run out should be clear.

COOK'S TIP

ROASTING CHICKEN IN AN OVEN THAT HAS NOT BEEN PRE-HEATED PRODUCES A PARTICULARLY CRISP SKIN.

TURKEY BREASTS WITH TOMATO-CORN SALSA

—

SALSA IN ALL ITS GUISES HAS TAKEN THE COUNTRY BY STORM. IT IS A VERSATILE, TASTY AND LOW FAT WAY TO SAUCE MEATS AND SEAFOOD. THIS SPICY VERSION TASTES BEST IN THE SUMMER, WHEN TOMATOES AND CORN ARE AT THEIR PEAK.

SERVES 4

4 skinless boneless turkey breast halves, about 6
    ounces each
2 tablespoons fresh lemon juice
2 tablespoons olive oil
½ teaspoon ground cumin
½ teaspoon dried oregano
1 teaspoon coarse black pepper
salt

FOR THE SALSA

1 fresh hot green chili pepper
1 pound tomatoes, seeded and chopped
1½ cups corn kernels, freshly cooked or thawed
    frozen
3 scallions, chopped
1 tablespoon chopped fresh parsley
2 tablespoons chopped fresh cilantro
2 tablespoons fresh lemon juice
3 tablespoons olive oil
1 teaspoon salt

With a mallet, pound the turkey breasts between 2 sheets of wax paper until thin. In a shallow dish, combine the lemon juice, oil, cumin, oregano, and pepper. Add the turkey and turn to coat. Cover and let stand at least 2 hours, or refrigerate overnight.

For the salsa, roast the chili over a gas flame, holding it with tongs, until charred on all sides. (Alternatively, char the skin under the broiler.) Let cool 5 minutes. Wearing rubber gloves, carefully rub off the charred skin. For a less hot flavor, also discard the white seeds. Chop the chili into fine pieces and place in a bowl.

Add the remaining salsa ingredients to the chili and toss well to blend. Set aside.

Remove the turkey from the marinade. Season lightly on both sides with salt to taste.

Heat a ridged grill pan. When hot, add the turkey breasts and cook until browned, about 3 minutes. Turn and cook the meat on the other side until it is cooked through, 3-4 minutes more. Serve the turkey immediately, accompanied by salsa.

VARIATION

USE THE COOKED TURKEY, THINLY SLICED AND COMBINED WITH THE SALSA, AS A FILLING FOR WARMED FLOUR TORTILLAS.

PORK CHOPS WITH SOUR GREEN CHILI SALSA

—

THIS TART AND TERRIFIC SALSA PROVIDES A PERFECT ACCENT TO BROILED PORK CHOPS. GRILL
THEM OUTSIDE IF THE WEATHER PERMITS.

SERVES 4

2 tablespoons vegetable oil

1 tablespoon fresh lemon juice

2 teaspoons ground cumin

1 teaspoon dried oregano

salt and pepper

8 pork loin chops, about ¾ inch thick

FOR THE SALSA

2 fresh hot green chili peppers

2 green bell peppers, seeded and chopped

1 tomato, peeled and seeded

½ onion, coarsely chopped

4 scallions

1 pickled jalapeño, stem removed

2 tablespoons olive oil

2 tablespoons fresh lime juice

3 tablespoons cider vinegar

1 teaspoon salt

In a small bowl, combine the vegetable oil, lemon juice, cumin, and oregano. Add pepper to taste and stir to blend.

Arrange the pork chops in one layer in a shallow dish. Brush each with the oil mixture on both sides. Cover and let stand 2-3 hours, or refrigerate overnight.

For the salsa, roast the chilies over a gas flame, holding them with tongs, until charred on all sides. (Alternatively, char the skins under the broiler.) Let cool 5 minutes. Wearing rubber gloves, remove the charred skin. For a less hot flavor, discard the seeds.

Place the chilies in a food processor or blender. Add the remaining salsa ingredients. Process until finely chopped; do not purée.

Transfer the salsa to a heavy saucepan and simmer 15 minutes, stirring occasionally. Set aside.

Season the pork chops. Heat a ridged grill pan. (Alternatively, preheat the broiler.) When hot, add the pork chops and cook until browned, about 5 minutes. Turn and continue cooking until done, 5-7 minutes more. Work in batches, if necessary.

Serve the chops immediately, with the sour green chili salsa on the side.

PORK FAJITAS

HERE'S ANOTHER GREAT BARBECUE DISH. FAJITAS HAVE ALWAYS BEEN SERVED AT PARTIES IN TEXAS AND THE SOUTHWEST; THEY ARE EASY TO PREPARE AND FUN TO EAT. SLICED BREAST OF CHICKEN OR STRIP STEAK ARE ALSO EXCELLENT FAJITA FILLINGS.

34

SERVES 6

juice of 3 limes

6 tablespoons olive oil

1 teaspoon dried oregano

1 teaspoon ground cumin

½ teaspoon red pepper flakes

1½ pounds pork tenderloin, cut across in 3-inch
*   pieces*

salt and pepper

2 large onions, halved and thinly sliced

1 large green bell pepper, seeded and thinly sliced
*   lengthwise*

FOR SERVING

12-15 flour tortillas, warmed

tomato salsa

guacamole

sour cream

In a shallow dish, combine the lime juice, 3 tablespoons of the oil, the oregano, cumin, and red pepper flakes and mix well. Add the pork pieces and turn to coat. Cover and let stand 1 hour.

Remove the pieces of pork from the marinade. Pat them dry and season with salt and pepper.

Heat a ridged grill pan. When hot, add the pork and cook over high heat, turning occasionally, until browned on all sides and cooked through, about 10-12 minutes.

Meanwhile, heat the remaining oil in a large skillet. Add the onions and bell pepper. Stir in ½ teaspoon salt and cook until the vegetables are very soft, about 15 minutes (see above). Stir occasionally. Remove from the heat and set aside.

Slice the pork pieces into thin strips. Add to the onion mixture and reheat briefly if necessary.

Spoon a little of the pork mixture onto each tortilla. Garnish with salsa, guacamole, and sour cream, and roll up. Alternatively, the fajitas may be assembled at the table.

TAMALE PIE

—

THIS IS A SUBLIME, SUPER SPICY TEXAS VERSION OF SHEPHERD'S PIE. ONCE YOU HAVE TRIED
IT YOU'LL NEVER GO BACK TO THE OLD VERSION.

36

SERVES 8

4 ounces bacon, chopped

1 onion, minced

1 pound lean ground beef

2-3 teaspoons chili powder

1 teaspoon salt

2 cups peeled fresh or canned tomatoes

⅓ cup chopped black olives

*1 cup corn kernels, freshly cooked or thawed
frozen*

½ cup sour cream

*1 cup shredded Monterey
Jack cheese*

FOR THE TAMALE CRUST

1-1¼ cups chicken stock

salt and pepper

1½ cups masa harina or cornmeal

6 tablespoons margarine or shortening

½ teaspoon baking powder

¼ cup milk

Preheat the oven to 375°F.

Cook the bacon in a large skillet until the fat is rendered, 2-3 minutes. Pour off excess fat, leaving 1-2 tablespoons. Add the onion and cook until just softened, about 5 minutes.

Add the beef, chili powder, and salt and cook 5 minutes, stirring to break up the meat. Stir in the tomatoes and cook 5 minutes more, breaking them up with a spoon.

Add the olives, corn, and sour cream, and mix well. Transfer to a 15-inch-long rectangular or oval baking dish. Set aside.

For the crust, bring the stock to a boil in a saucepan; season it with a little salt and pepper if necessary.

In a food processor, combine the masa harina or cornmeal, margarine or shortening, baking powder, and milk. Process until combined. With the machine on, gradually pour in the hot stock until a smooth, thick batter is obtained. If the batter becomes too thick to spread, thin out by adding additional hot stock or water, a little at a time.

Pour the batter over the top of the beef mixture, spreading it evenly with a metal spatula.

Bake until the top is just browned, about 20 minutes. Sprinkle the surface evenly with the shredded cheese and continue baking until melted and bubbling, 10-15 minutes more. Serve immediately.

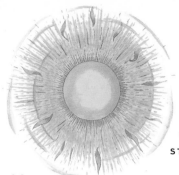

BEEF ENCHILADAS

—

THESE DELICIOUS STUFFED AND ROLLED TORTILLAS CAN BE VARIED
ALMOST INFINITELY. ONCE YOU HAVE MASTERED THIS RECIPE, TRY
STUFFING THEM WITH PORK, CHICKEN, TURKEY, CHEESE OR SHRIMP.

SERVES 4

2 pounds chuck steak

1 tablespoon vegetable oil, plus more for frying

1 teaspoon salt

1 teaspoon dried oregano

½ teaspoon ground cumin

1 onion, quartered

2 garlic cloves, crushed

4 cups enchilada sauce

12 corn tortillas

1 cup shredded Monterey Jack cheese

FOR SERVING

chopped scallions

sour cream

Preheat the oven to 325°F.

Place the meat on a sheet of foil. Rub all over with the oil. Sprinkle both sides with the salt, oregano, and cumin and rub in well. Add the onion and garlic. Top with more foil and roll up to seal the edges, leaving room for some steam expansion.

Place in a baking dish. Bake until the meat is tender enough to shred, about 3 hours. Remove the meat from the foil and roughly shred with a fork.

Add ½ cup of the enchilada sauce to the beef. Stir well. Spoon a thin layer of enchilada sauce on the bottom of a rectangular baking dish, or in 4 individual baking dishes.

Place the remaining enchilada sauce in a skillet and warm gently.

Put a ½ inch layer of vegetable oil in a second skillet and heat until hot but not smoking. With tongs, lower a tortilla into the oil; the temperature is correct if it just sizzles.

Cook 2 seconds, then turn and cook the other side 2 seconds. Lift out, drain over the skillet, and then transfer to the skillet of sauce. Dip in the sauce just to coat both sides.

Transfer the softened tortilla immediately to a plate. Spread 2-3 spoonfuls of the beef mixture down the center of the tortilla. Roll up and place seam-side down in the prepared dish. Repeat the process for the remaining tortillas.

Spoon the remaining sauce from the skillet over the enchiladas, spreading it to the ends. Sprinkle the cheese down the center.

Bake until the cheese just melts, 10-15 minutes. Sprinkle with chopped scallions and serve at once, with sour cream on the side.

BLACK BEAN CHILI

—

THERE ARE PROBABLY AS MANY CHILI RECIPES IN AMERICA AS THERE ARE "KISS ME I'M THE CHEF" APRONS. THIS ONE USES BLACK BEANS AND IS GARNISHED WITH FRESH CILANTRO.

SERVES 6

2 cups dried black beans, soaked overnight and
  drained
2 tablespoons coarse salt
2 tablespoons vegetable oil
2 onions, chopped
1 green bell pepper, seeded and chopped
2 garlic cloves, minced
2 pounds ground chuck steak
1½ tablespoons ground
  cumin
½ teaspoon cayenne
2½ teaspoons paprika
2 tablespoons dried
  oregano
1 teaspoon salt
3 tablespoons tomato paste
3 cups chopped peeled, fresh or canned tomatoes
½ cup red wine
1 bay leaf

FOR SERVING

chopped fresh cilantro
sour cream
shredded Monterey Jack or cheddar cheese

Put the beans in a large pot. Add fresh cold water to cover. Bring to a boil, then cover and simmer 30 minutes. Add the coarse salt and continue simmering until the beans are tender, about 30 minutes or longer. Drain and set aside.

Heat the oil in a large saucepan or flameproof casserole. Add the onions and bell pepper. Cook the vegetables over medium heat until just softened, about 5 minutes, stirring occasionally. Stir in the garlic and continue cooking 1 minute more.

Add the beef and cook over high heat, stirring frequently, until browned and crumbly. Reduce the heat and stir in the cumin, cayenne, paprika, oregano, and salt.

Add the tomato paste, tomatoes, drained black beans, wine, and bay leaf and stir well. Simmer 20 minutes, stirring occasionally.

Taste for seasoning. Remove the bay leaf and serve immediately, with chopped fresh cilantro, sour cream, and shredded cheese.

COOK'S TIP

USE A LARGE POT TO SOAK THE BEANS IN OVERNIGHT AS THEY ARE LIKELY TO INCREASE IN VOLUME.

LONE STAR STEAK AND POTATO DINNER

—

THIS BIG HEARTY RIB-STICKING MEAL TASTES AS GOOD IN THE KITCHEN AS IT DOES OUT
ON THE RANGE.

42

SERVES 4

3 tablespoons olive oil

5 large garlic cloves, minced

1 teaspoon coarse black pepper

½ teaspoon ground allspice

1 teaspoon ground cumin

½ teaspoon chili powder

2 teaspoons dried oregano

1 tablespoon cider vinegar

4 boneless sirloin steaks,
about ¾ inch thick

salt

FOR THE POTATOES

¼ cup vegetable oil

1 onion, chopped

1 teaspoon salt

2 pounds potatoes, boiled and diced

2-5 tablespoons chopped canned green chilies,
according to taste

FOR SERVING

tomato salsa

freshly cooked corn-on-the-cob
(optional)

Heat the olive oil in a heavy skillet. When hot, add the garlic and cook, stirring often, until tender and just brown, about 3 minutes; do not let the garlic burn.

Transfer the garlic and oil to a shallow dish large enough to hold the steaks in one layer.

Add the pepper, spices, herbs, and vinegar to the garlic and blend thoroughly. If necessary, add just enough water to obtain a moderately thick paste.

Add the steaks to the dish and turn to coat evenly on both sides with the spice mixture. Cover and let stand 2 hours, or refrigerate the steaks overnight. (Bring them to room temperature before cooking.)

For the potatoes, heat the oil in a large nonstick skillet. Add the onion and salt. Cook over medium heat until softened, about 5 minutes. Add the potatoes and chilies. Cook, stirring occasionally, until well browned, 15-20 minutes.

Season the steaks on both sides with salt to taste. Heat a ridged grill pan. When hot, add the steaks and cook, turning once, until done to your taste. Allow about 2 minutes on each side for medium-rare; and 3-4 minutes for well done.

If necessary, briefly reheat the potatoes and serve with the tomato salsa and corn, if using.

GUACAMOLE

—

NOTHING USHERS IN A SOUTHWESTERN MEAL
BETTER THAN SPICY, CREAMY GUACAMOLE.

44

MAKES 2 CUPS

3 large ripe avocados

3 scallions, minced

1 garlic clove, minced

1 tablespoon olive oil

1 tablespoon sour cream

½ teaspoon salt

2 tablespoons fresh lemon or lime juice

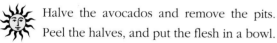 Halve the avocados and remove the pits. Peel the halves, and put the flesh in a bowl. With a fork, mash the avocado flesh coarsely.

Add the scallions, garlic, olive oil, sour cream, salt, and lemon or lime juice. Mash until well blended, but do not overwork the mixture. Small chunks of avocado should still remain. Taste the guacamole and adjust the seasoning if necessary, with more salt or lemon or lime juice.

Transfer to a serving bowl. Serve immediately.

COOK'S TIP

GUACAMOLE DOES NOT KEEP WELL, BUT, IF NECESSARY, IT CAN BE STORED IN THE REFRIGERATOR FOR A FEW HOURS. COVER THE SURFACE WITH PLASTIC WRAP.

TOMATO SALSA

—

ALTHOUGH STOREBOUGHT SALSA CAN BE VERY
GOOD, WHY NOT TRY MAKING YOUR OWN?

MAKES 3½ CUPS

1 fresh hot green chili pepper, seeded if desired, chopped

1 garlic clove, coarsely chooped

½ red onion, coarsely chopped

3 scallions, chopped

¼ cup fresh cilantro leaves

1½ pounds ripe tomatoes, seeded and coarsely chopped

1-3 canned green chilies, according to taste

1 tablespoon olive oil

2 tablespoons fresh lime or lemon juice

½ teaspoon salt, or to taste

2-3 tablespoons tomato juice or cold water

In a food processor or blender, combine the fresh green chili, garlic, red onion, scallions, and cilantro. Process until finely chopped.

Add the tomatoes, canned chilies, olive oil, lime or lemon juice, salt, and tomato juice or water. Pulse on and off until just chopped; the salsa should be chunky and not too smooth.

Transfer to a bowl and taste for seasoning. Let stand at least 30 minutes before serving. This salsa is best served the day it is made.

BEAN DIP

—

SERVE THIS VERSATILE DIP WITH THE MANY DELICIOUS VARIETIES OF CHIPS AVAILABLE.

MAKES 3 CUPS

*1½ cups dried pinto beans, soaked overnight and
    drained*

1 bay leaf

3 tablespoons coarse salt

1 tablespoon vegetable oil

1 small onion, sliced

1 garlic clove, minced

2-4 canned hot green chilies (optional)

⅓ cup sour cream, plus more for garnishing

½ teaspoon ground cumin

hot pepper sauce

1 tablespoon chopped fresh cilantro

tortilla chips, for serving

Place the beans in a large pot. Add fresh cold water to cover and the bay leaf. Bring to a boil, then cover, and simmer 30 minutes.

Add the coarse salt and continue simmering until the beans are tender, about 30 minutes or more.

Drain the beans, reserving ½ cup of the cooking liquid. Let cool slightly. Discard the bay leaf.

Heat the oil in a nonstick skillet. Add the onion and garlic and cook over low heat until they have just softened, 8-10 minutes, stirring occasionally.

In a food processor or blender, combine the beans, onion mixture, chilies if using, and the reserved cooking liquid. Process until the mixture resembles a coarse purée.

Transfer to a bowl and stir in the sour cream, cumin, and hot pepper sauce to taste (see above). Stir in the cilantro, garnish with sour cream, and serve warm, with tortilla chips.

COOK'S TIP

TRY THIS DISH WITH JALAPEÑO PEPPERS, SOUR CREAM, GUACAMOLE AND TORTILLA CHIPS.

TOMATO RICE

FRESH TOMATOES ARE BEST IN THIS TASTY DISH,
BUT CANNED WILL DO IN A PINCH. COLD LEFTOVERS
CAN BE TRANSFORMED INTO A SAVORY SALAD.

48

SERVES 4

2 cups unsalted chicken or beef stock

1½ tablespoons vegetable oil

1 small onion, minced

1 cup long-grain rice

1 teaspoon salt

½ teaspoon ground cumin

*1 medium-size tomato, peeled, seeded, and
    chopped*

1 tablespoon tomato paste

1 tablespoon chopped fresh cilantro

Place the stock in a saucepan and heat until just simmering. Remove from the heat, cover, and set aside.

Heat the oil in a large heavy saucepan. Add the onion and rice and cook over medium heat until the onion is just softened, about 5 minutes. Stir in the salt, cumin, tomato, and tomato paste and cook 1 minute more, stirring all the time.

Gradually stir in the warm stock. Bring to a boil, then lower heat, cover, and cook until the rice is tender and all the liquid is absorbed, 30-40 minutes.

Fluff the rice with a fork and stir in the cilantro. Serve immediately.

ENCHILADA SAUCE

MAKE A BIG BATCH OF THIS SMOOTH SPICY SAUCE;
IT TRADITIONALLY TOPS ENCHILADAS BUT ALSO
GOES WELL WITH BURRITOS AND TACOS.

MAKES ABOUT 6 CUPS

4 16-ounce cans peeled plum tomatoes, drained

3 garlic cloves, coarsely chopped

1 onion, coarsely chopped

2-4 tablespoons ground red chili

1 teaspoon cayenne, or to taste

1 teaspoon ground cumin

½ teaspoon dried oregano

½ teaspoon salt

1 cup water

In a food processor or blender, combine the tomatoes, garlic, and onion. Process until smooth.

Pour and scrape the mixture into a heavy saucepan.

Add the remaining ingredients and stir to blend. Bring to a boil, stirring occasionally. Boil 2-3 minutes. Reduce the heat, cover, and simmer 15 minutes.

Dilute with ½-1 cup water, as necessary, to obtain a pouring consistency. Taste for seasoning; if a hotter sauce is desired, add more cayenne, rather than more ground chili.

SANTA FE SHRIMP SALAD

—

THE CONTRAST OF BRIGHT PINK SHRIMP AND GREEN LETTUCE GIVE THIS COOL CRISP SALAD GREAT VISUAL APPEAL. YOU CAN ADD LOBSTER, CRAB OR SCALLOPS IF YOU ARE FEELING EXTRAVAGANT.

SERVES 4

1 pound cooked peeled shrimp

2 scallions, chopped

2 tablespoons fresh lemon juice

2 tablespoons extra-virgin olive oil

1 teaspoon salt

6 cups shredded lettuce

1 large ripe avocado

1 cup tomato salsa

FOR GARNISHING

fresh cilantro sprigs

lime slices

In a bowl, combine the shrimp, scallions, lemon juice, oil, and salt (see above right). Mix well and set aside.

Line 4 plates (or a large platter) with the shredded lettuce.

Halve the avocado and remove the pit. With a small melon baller, scoop out balls of avocado and add to the shrimp mixture. Scrape the remaining avocado flesh into the salad and stir. Add the salsa to the shrimp mixture and stir gently to blend.

Divide the shrimp mixture among the plates, piling it in the center. Garnish each salad with fresh cilantro sprigs and slices of lime.

Serve immediately.

COOK'S TIP

TO DEVEIN SHRIMPS, FIRST PEEL AWAY THE SHELL FROM THE BODY. WHEN YOU REACH THE TAIL HOLD THE BODY AND PULL AWAY THE TAIL; THE SHELL WILL COME OFF WITH IT. MAKE A SHALLOW CUT DOWN THE CENTRE OF THE CURVED BACK OF THE SHRIMP. PULL OUT THE BLACK VEIN WITH A COCKTAIL STICK OR YOUR FINGERS.

PINTO BEAN SALAD

—

SERVE THIS HEARTY SALAD WITH GRILLED CHICKEN OR FISH. IT ALSO MAKES A GREAT ADDITION
TO A BUFFET OR BARBECUE.

52

SERVES 4

1½ cups dried pinto beans, soaked overnight and
    drained
1 bay leaf
3 tablespoons coarse salt
2 ripe tomatoes, diced
4 scallions, minced

FOR THE DRESSING
¼ cup fresh lemon juice
salt and pepper
6 tablespoons olive oil
1 garlic clove, minced
3 tablespoons chopped fresh cilantro

Put the beans in a large pot. Add fresh cold
water to cover and add the bay leaf. Bring to
a boil, then cover, and simmer 30 minutes. Add the salt and continue
simmering until tender, about
30 minutes more. Drain
and allow to cool
slightly. Discard the
bay leaf.

For the dressing,

mix the lemon juice and 1 teaspoon salt with a fork
until dissolved. Gradually stir in the oil until thick.
Add the garlic, cilantro, and pepper to taste.

While the beans are still warm, place them in a
large bowl. Add the dressing and toss to coat. Let
the beans cool completely.

Add the tomatoes and scallions and toss to coat
evenly (see above). Stand for 30 minutes and serve.

COOK'S TIP

A QUICKER ALTERNATIVE TO SOAKING BEANS OVERNIGHT
IS TO PUT THE DRIED BEANS IN A LARGE PAN OF WATER,
BRING TO THE BOIL AND BOIL FOR 20 MINUTES, THEN
LEAVE THEM TO SOAK FOR 1 HOUR.

HAM AND BLACK-EYED PEA SALAD

BLACK-EYED PEAS ARE TRADITIONALLY SERVED ON NEW YEAR'S DAY FOR GOOD LUCK IN THE COMING YEAR, BUT THIS SALAD TASTES DELICIOUS ALL YEAR ROUND.

SERVES 8

1 cup dry black-eyed peas

1 onion, peeled

1 carrot, peeled

½ pound smoked ham, diced

3 medium tomatoes, peeled, seeded, and diced (about 1 cup)

salt and pepper

FOR THE DRESSING

2 garlic cloves, minced

3 tablespoons olive oil

3 tablespoons red wine vinegar

2 tablespoons corn oil

1 tablespoon fresh lemon juice

1 tablespoon chopped fresh basil or 1 teaspoon dried basil

1 tablespoon whole-grain mustard

1 teaspoon soy sauce

½ teaspoon dried oregano

½ teaspoon sugar

¼ teaspoon Worcestershire sauce

½ teaspoon hot pepper sauce

 Soak the black-eyed peas in water to cover overnight. Drain.

Put the peas in a large saucepan and add the onion and carrot. Cover with fresh cold water and bring to a boil. Lower the heat and simmer until the peas are tender, about 1 hour. Drain, reserving the onion and carrot. Transfer the peas to a salad bowl.

Finely chop the onion and carrot. Toss with the peas. Stir in the ham and tomatoes.

For the dressing combine all the ingredients in a small bowl and whisk to mix.

Pour the dressing over the peas (see above). Season with salt and pepper to taste and then toss to combine.

VARIATION

FOR ITALIAN BEAN SALAD, USE CANNELLINI BEANS INSTEAD OF BLACK-EYED PEAS.

54

NEW MEXICO CHRISTMAS BISCOCHITOS

—

THE HOLIDAY SEASON IN NEW MEXICO IS ESPECIALLY BEAUTIFUL, WITH COLD CLEAR NIGHTS LIT BY STUBBY CANDLES IN PAPER BAGS LINED UP ALONG ROADSIDES, WALLS, ROOFS, AND WINDOWS. THESE CRISP COOKIES ARE AN ESSENTIAL PART OF THAT FESTIVE TIME.

MAKES 24

1½ cups flour

1 teaspoon baking powder

⅛ teaspoon salt

½ cup (1 stick) unsalted butter, at room temperature

½ cup sugar

1 egg

1 teaspoon whole aniseed

1 tablespoon brandy

¼ cup sugar mixed with ½ teaspoon ground cinnamon, for sprinkling

 Sift together the flour, baking powder, and salt. Set aside.

Beat the butter with the sugar until soft and fluffy. Add the egg, aniseed, and brandy and beat until incorporated. Fold in the dry ingredients just until blended to a dough. Refrigerate for at least 30 minutes.

Preheat the oven to 350°F. Grease 2 cookie sheets.

On a lightly floured surface, roll out the

chilled cookie dough to about ⅛ inch thickness.

With a cutter, pastry wheel, or knife, cut out the cookies into squares, diamonds, or other shapes. The traditional shape for biscochitos is a fleur-de-lis.

Place on the prepared cookie sheets and sprinkle lightly with the cinnamon sugar (see above).

Bake until just barely golden, about 10 minutes. Cool on the sheets 5 minutes before transferring to a wire rack to cool completely. The cookies can be kept in an airtight container for up to 1 week.

COOK'S TIP

IF DESIRED, THE PASTRY CAN BE MADE UP TO 2 DAYS IN ADVANCE AND REFRIGERATED.

CHOCOLATE CINNAMON CAKE WITH BANANA SAUCE

—

THIS EXOTIC TWIST ON A CLASSIC CHOCOLATE CAKE IS A REAL PALATE PLEASER. THE CREAMY
BANANA SAUCE IS A PERFECT COUNTERPART TO THE RICH CHOCOLATE FLAVOR.

SERVES 6

*4 1-ounce squares semisweet chocolate, finely
  chopped*
*½ cup (1 stick) unsalted butter, at room
  temperature*
1 tablespoon instant coffee powder
5 eggs, separated
1 cup granulated sugar
1 cup flour
2 teaspoons ground cinnamon

FOR THE SAUCE

4 ripe bananas
¼ cup light brown sugar, firmly packed
1 tablespoon fresh lemon juice
¾ cup whipping cream
1 tablespoon rum (optional)

 Preheat the oven to 350°F. Grease an 8-inch
round cake pan.

Combine the chocolate and butter in the top of a
double boiler or in a heatproof bowl set over hot
water. Stir until melted. Remove from the heat and
stir in the coffee. Set aside.

Beat the egg yolks with the granulated sugar

until thick and lemon-colored. Add the chocolate
mixture and beat on low speed just to blend the
mixtures evenly.

Sift together the flour and cinnamon into
a bowl.

In another bowl, beat the egg whites
until they hold stiff peaks.

Fold a dollop of whites into the
chocolate mixture to lighten it. Fold
in the remaining whites in 3 batches,
alternating with the sifted flour.

Pour the batter into the prepared pan. Bake
until a cake tester inserted in the center comes out
clean, approximately 40-50 minutes. Carefully
unmold the cake onto a wire rack.

Preheat the broiler.

For the sauce, slice the bananas into a shallow,
heatproof dish. Add the brown sugar and lemon
juice and stir to blend. Place under the broiler and
cook, stirring occasionally, until the sugar is
caramelized and bubbling, about 8 minutes.

Transfer the bananas to a bowl and mash with a
fork until almost smooth. Stir in the whipping cream
and rum, if using.

Serve the cake and sauce warm.

MEXICAN HOT FUDGE SUNDAES

—

CINNAMON AND COFFEE SPICE UP THIS HEAVENLY MOUNTAIN OF ICE CREAM AND HOT FUDGE.
THERE IS NO NEED TO SERVE ESPRESSO COFFEE WITH THIS DESSERT.

60

SERVES 4

1 pint vanilla ice cream
1 pint coffee ice cream
2 large ripe bananas, sliced
whipped cream
toasted sliced almonds

FOR THE SAUCE

¼ cup light brown sugar, firmly packed
½ cup light corn syrup
3 tablespoons strong black coffee
1 teaspoon ground cinnamon
5 1-ounce squares bittersweet chocolate, broken up
⅓ cup whipping cream
3 tablespoons coffee liqueur (optional)

For the sauce, combine the brown sugar, corn syrup, coffee, and cinnamon in a heavy saucepan. Bring to a boil. Boil the mixture, stirring constantly, about 5 minutes.

Remove from the heat and stir in the chocolate. When melted and smooth, stir in the cream and liqueur, if using. Let the sauce cool just to lukewarm, or if

made ahead, reheat gently while assembling the sundaes.

Fill sundae dishes with 1 scoop each of vanilla and coffee ice cream.

Arrange the bananas on the top of each dish (see above). Pour the warm sauce over the bananas, then top each sundae with a generous rosette of whipped cream.

COOK'S TIP

IF PREFERRED, USE MILK CHOCOLATE INSTEAD OF BITTERSWEET, BUT TASTE BEFORE SERVING.

PUEBLO PASTELITOS

—

THESE TINY FRUIT FILLED BITES ARE IRRESISTIBLE. VARY THE FILLINGS WITH
THE WIDE RANGE OF DRIED FRUITS NOW AVAILABLE: BLUEBERRIES, STRAWBERRIES,
PEACHES OR PEARS.

MAKES 16

2 cups dried fruit, such as apricots or prunes

½ cup light brown sugar, firmly packed

½ cup raisins

½ cup pine nuts or chopped almonds

½ teaspoon ground cinnamon

oil for frying

3 tablespoons granulated sugar mixed with 1
   teaspoon ground cinnamon, for sprinkling

FOR THE PASTRY DOUGH

2 cups flour

¼ teaspoon baking powder

¼ teaspoon salt

2 teaspoons granulated sugar

4 tablespoons unsalted butter, chilled

2 tablespoons shortening

½-⅔ cup ice water

For the pastry dough, sift the flour, baking powder, salt, and sugar into a bowl. With a pastry blender or 2 knives, cut in the butter and shortening until the mixture resembles coarse meal. Sprinkle with ½ cup ice water and mix until the dough holds together. If the dough is too crumbly,

add a little more water, 1 tablespoon at a time.

Gather the dough into a ball and flatten into a disk. Wrap the dough in wax paper and refrigerate it at least 30 minutes.

Place the dried fruit in a saucepan and add enough cold water to cover. Bring to a boil, then simmer gently until the fruit is soft enough to purée, about 30 minutes.

Drain the fruit and place in a food processor or blender. Process until smooth. Return the fruit purée to the saucepan. Add the brown sugar and cook, stirring constantly, until thick, about 5 minutes. Remove from the heat and stir in the raisins, pine nuts or almonds, and cinnamon. Allow the mixture to cool.

On a lightly floured surface, roll out the chilled dough to about ⅛ inch thickness. Stamp out rounds with a 4-inch cookie cutter. (Roll and cut out in 2 batches if it is more convenient.)

Place a spoonful of the fruit filling in the center of each round.

Moisten the edge with a brush dipped in water, then fold over the dough to form a half-moon shape. With a fork, crimp the rounded edge.

Put a ½ inch layer of oil in a heavy skillet and

heat until hot but not smoking (to test, drop a scrap of dough in the oil; if the oil sizzles, it is hot enough). Add the turnovers, a few at a time, and fry until golden on both sides, 1½ minutes per side.

Drain briefly on paper towels, then sprinkle with the cinnamon sugar. Serve the pastelitos warm.

INDEX